To Brandy,
I wish you joy
and blessings
Author
T. Holmes
Maria

BEYOND THE MYTH

HOW TO LIVE THE LIFE YOU DESIRE

MARIA T. HOLMES

Copyright © 2010 by Maria Holmes

All rights reserved. No part of this book may be used or reproduced or transmitted in any form or by any means, electronic of mechanical, including photocopying, recording, or by an information storage system, without permission from the publisher.

First Edition

Get Published

Publishers Cataloging-in-Publication Data
Holmes, Maria
   Beyond the Myth: How to Live the Life You Desire / Maria Holmes – 1st ed.

p. cm.
ISBN-13: 979-0-9830946-0-9
1. Personal Development 2. Law of Attraction

To: _____

From: _____

May the wonder
   the wisdom
      and the understanding
of this book bring
   joy to your soul
      and joy to your life.

— Maria Holmes

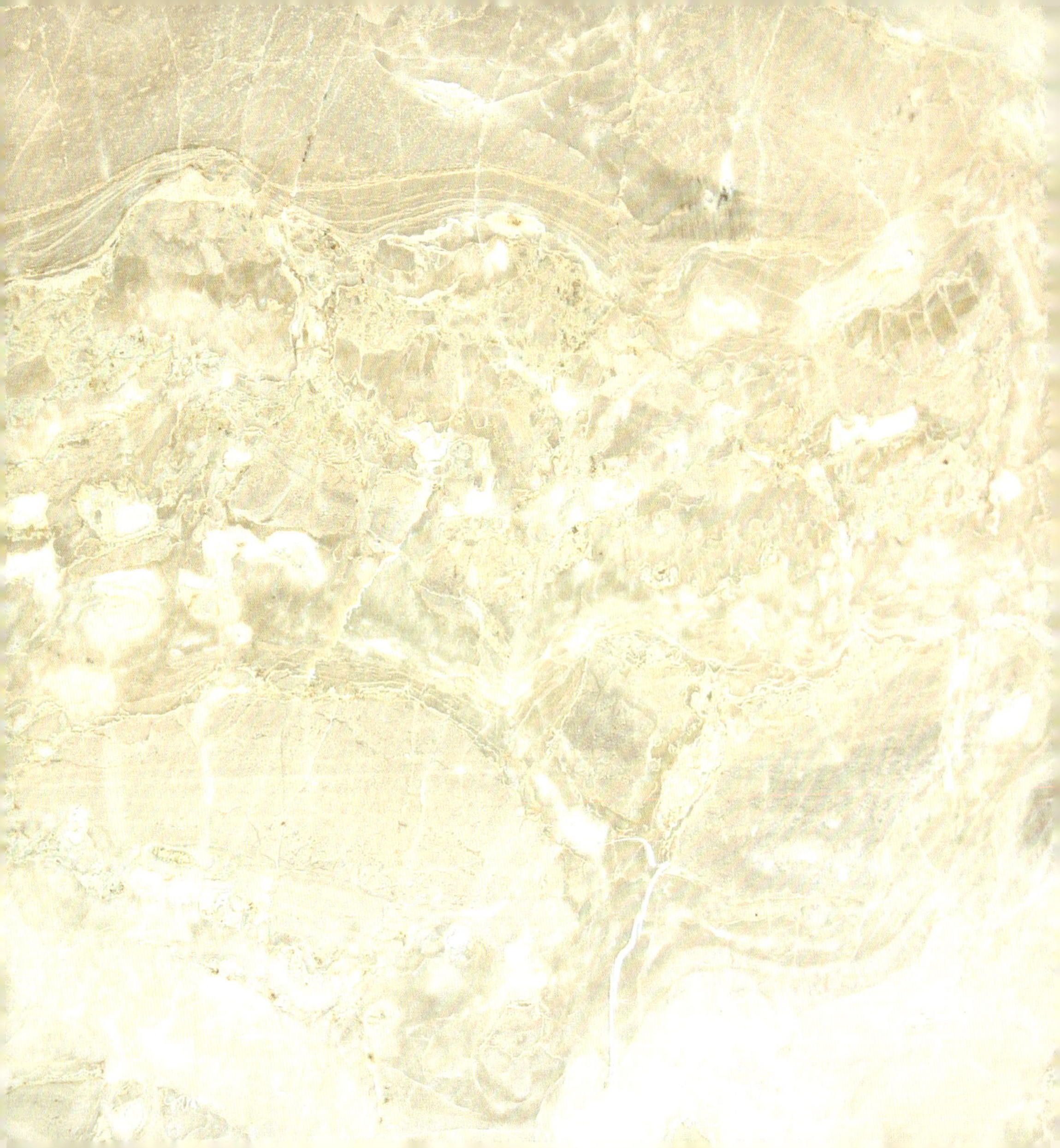

Contents

Chapter 1: Possibility   11

Chapter 2: Create   17

Chapter 3: Attract   25

Chapter 4: Choice   45

Chapter 5: Manifest   51

Chapter 6: Results   55

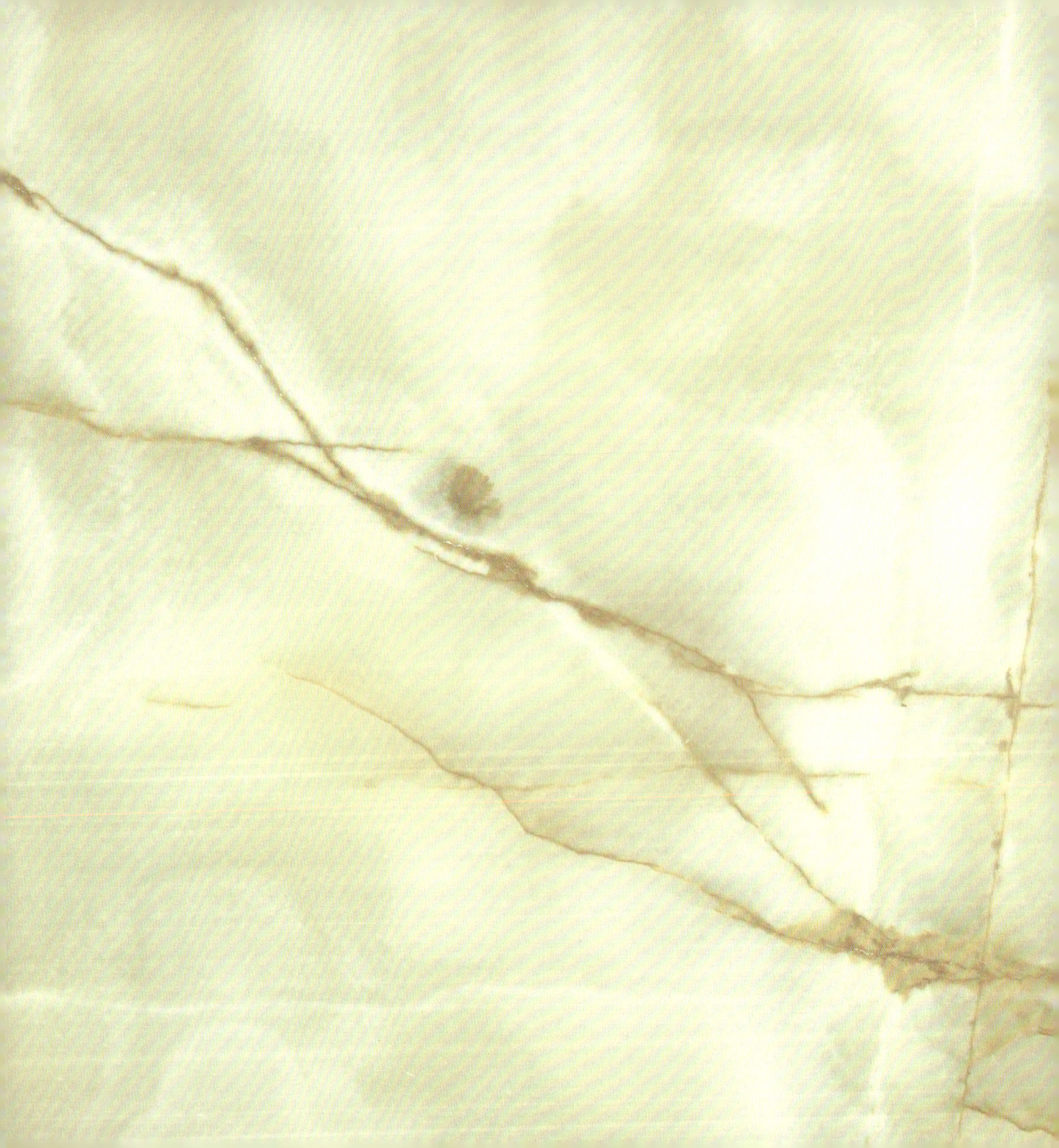

Acknowledgments

My special thanks to my mentor and teacher, Bob Proctor, for the awareness, the insight, and the knowledge this material has brought into my life. I want to thank Laura Cross for the support and the understanding to see me through this project. I want to thank my coach, Roger McKinley. Thank you, Carol Gates, for seeing me though the LifeSuccess Coaching program. Thank you to my Mastermind Group for allowing me to learn from you: Henry Martens, Chris Hassall, Dennis Klinsky, Tarıg Johnson, Joanna Shaw, and Anda Tudor. And finally to my daughter, Sandra Holmes; grandson, Sebastion Holmes; and sister, Martha Hicks, for your loving hearts that have enriched my life in more ways than I could have ever imagined— Thank you.

You cannot do a kindness too soon for you never know how soon it will be too late

— Ralph Waldo Emerson

Chapter 1 | Possibility

Awaken and See the Possibilities in the World around You.

The Universe is made up of energy. It moves all around us and through us, linking everything we do, say, think, and feel with many other people, in many other places. Many of us go through our entire lives without ever becoming aware that this energy is the true nature of the Universe. Once you do, however, you will have an enormous resource at your disposal that can make it possible for you to realize your dreams. All of them.

I remember the first time my eyes were opened to the way in which all of the energy in the Universe is connected and how I am connected to

Cherish your visions
and your dreams
As they are the
children of your soul
The blueprints of your
ultimate achievements
— Napoleon Hill

all of it in turn. I was rushing, trying to catch my flight from Toronto to Chicago, and completely caught up in the stresses of my own little world. My mind was full of all of the things I needed to do — mundane tasks, but when you are in that type of mindset, every little thing seems overly important.

The night was cool and the sky was clear, and as I neared the terminal, I just happened to look up. And that's when it hit me. Hovering above me in the sky, I saw a stunningly clear blanket of stars. It took my breath away, and I could do nothing but stand and stare up at this essence of natural beauty. I thought I could almost feel the energy from those many stars reaching through the night air to touch me in that moment.

And indeed, that was exactly what was happening. It was not just a beautiful view I had suddenly become aware of. As I stood there, it hit me; there are 400 billion stars in our galaxy, and our galaxy is

To the mind that is still
The whole universe surrenders
— Chinese Proverb

only one of probably many millions in the Universe. Each of the stars in each of these galaxies is made up of energy — an energy that was reaching me at that moment through many layers of space and time.

As I was contemplating this cosmic energy, it also occurred to me our own human bodies are really made up of the same energy as those stars, just in a different form. After all, we are made up of cells, which in turn are made up of atoms. Atoms, of course, are composed of subatomic particles — essentially energy. The same particles that make up all the stars in the galaxy and all of the galaxies in the Universe are also what make up our bodies and our minds.

This was truly a life changing realization for me. As the days and weeks went by, I couldn't stop thinking about it. I read anything and everything I could get my hands on that described this type of relationship. And what I found was even more eye opening — The Law of Attraction.

*Life is an echo;
What you send out comes back*

— *Lao Tzu*

Chapter 2 | Create

Understand the Law of Attraction and Put it to Use in Your Own Life

Essentially, the Law of Attraction states: your thoughts directly shape the events which occur in your life. If you want something to happen and you are able to focus enough intellectual and emotional energy on it, you can make it so. Where you place your energy is where it manifests. If it is knowledge you need, you will attract it. If it is people you need, you will attract them. Whatever it is that you need, you will attract it. This is possible because the energy you give out is able to interact with the rest of the energy in the Universe to help you achieve whatever ends you hold most dear.

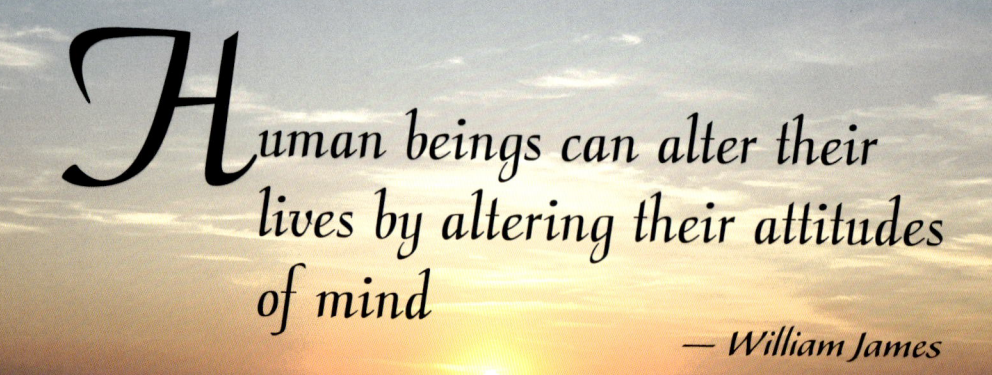

Human beings can alter their lives by altering their attitudes of mind

— William James

While the name was not attached to the principle until recently, the Law of Attraction has been significant throughout history — in various writings and teachings, and different cultures. In fact, scholars from all ages seem to have been fascinated with the idea of energies shared among all things in the Universe and the power our thoughts have to influence the interactions of these various energies.

Historical references include...

"Be careful how you think. Your life is shaped by your thoughts."
— From Proverbs 4:23 in the Good News Translation of the Bible

"Nothing is impossible in the mind. All its guidance and power are available to you. When you have fully realized thought causes all, you will know there will never be any limits that you yourself do not impose."
— U. S. Anderson

"The more one acts in harmony with the Universe, the more one will achieve with less effort."
— From the Tao Technique, a book which lays out the path one must follow to achieve inner strength and virtue and which dates from between 551 and 479 BC

We become what we think about

— *William James*

"The action of mind plants that nucleus which, if allowed to grow undisturbed, will eventually attract to itself all the conditions necessary for its manifestation in outward visible form."
— From Thomas Troward's The Edinburgh Lectures on Mental Science, given in 1904

"You are what you think, not what you think you are."
— From *Prosperity Through Thought Force* by Bruce MacLelland, published in 1907

"Every completed manifestation of whatever kind, and on whatever scale, is unquenchable energy of attraction that causes objects to steadily increase in power and definiteness of purpose, until the process of growth is completed and the matured form stands out as an accomplished fact."
— John Ambrose Fleming in 1902

"All matter originates and exists only by virtue of a force which brings the particle of an atom to vibration and holds this most minute solar system of the atom together. We must assume behind this force the existence of a conscious and intelligent mind. This mind is the matrix of all matter."
— From *The Nature of Matter,* a speech given in 1944 by German physicist Max Planck

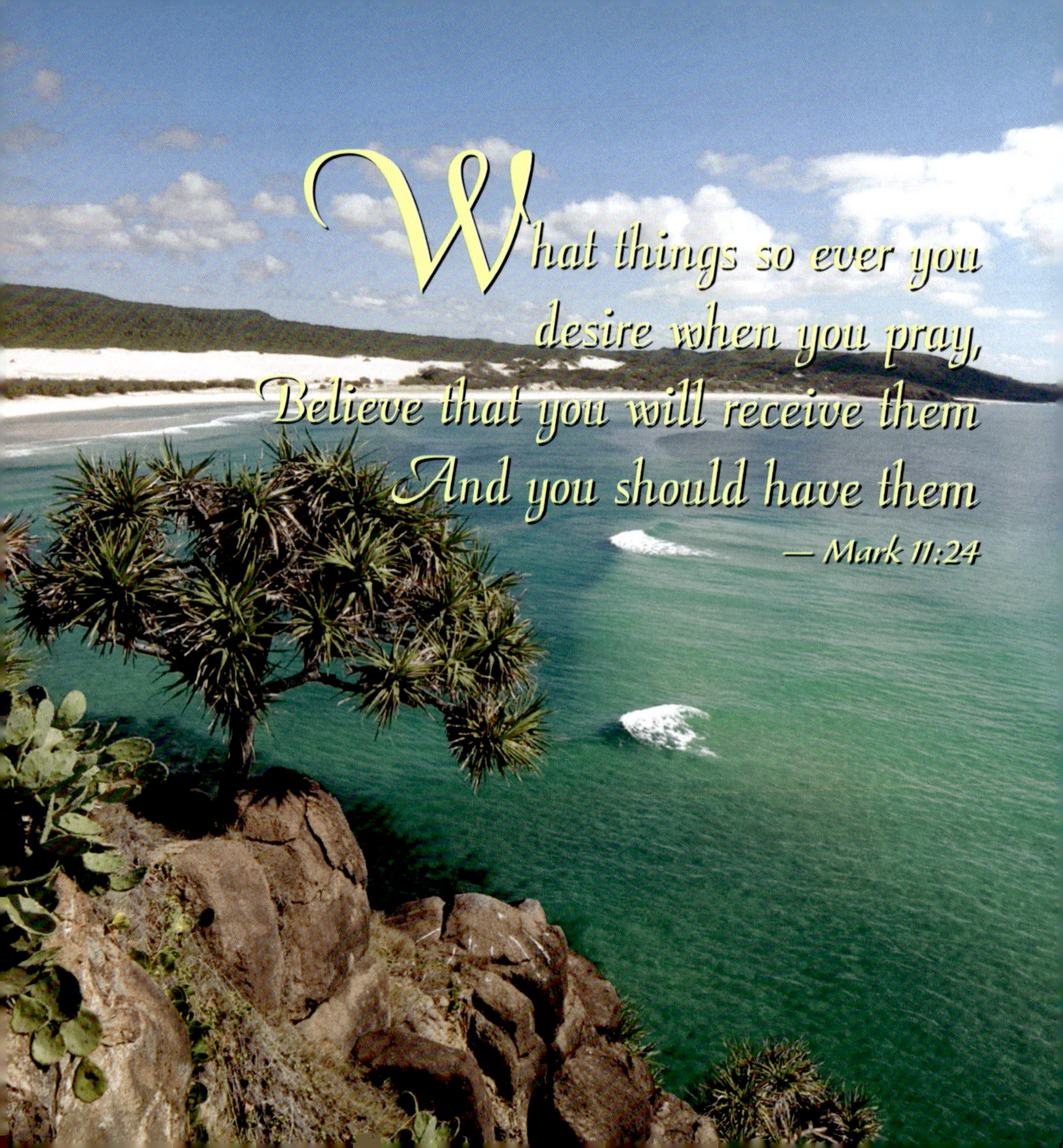
What things so ever you
desire when you pray,
Believe that you will receive them
And you should have them
— Mark 11:24

"A human being is part of a whole, called by us Universe, a part limited in time and space. He experiences himself, his thoughts and feelings, as something separated from the rest, a kind of optical delusion of his consciousness. This delusion is a kind of prison for us, restricting us to our personal desires and to affection for a few persons nearest us. Our task must be to free ourselves from this prison by widening our circles of compassion to embrace all living creatures and the whole of nature in its beauty."

— Albert Einstein

As you can see, many great thinkers of the ages were convinced our thoughts were capable of effecting the most dramatic changes in the Universe around us. Indeed, many held that this was the only way in which change could occur. They truly believed we could each shape our own destiny by claiming possession of our energies and directing them harmoniously with the other energies all around us. We are the masters of our own destinies. We have only to realize the potential, which lies within us.

All that we are is a result of what we thought

— *Buddha*

Chapter 3 | Attract

The Principles of the Law of Attraction

There are many different elements that make up the theory and premise of the Law of Attraction, but they all come back to the same basic truth. You can determine the shape of your future if you truly believe you can <u>and</u> if you keep your thoughts focused in the right direction.

Desire

Desire is the starting point of all achievement and the cornerstone that all the other principles build upon. In this context, Desire is the thought you have when you picture the outcome you want to effect.

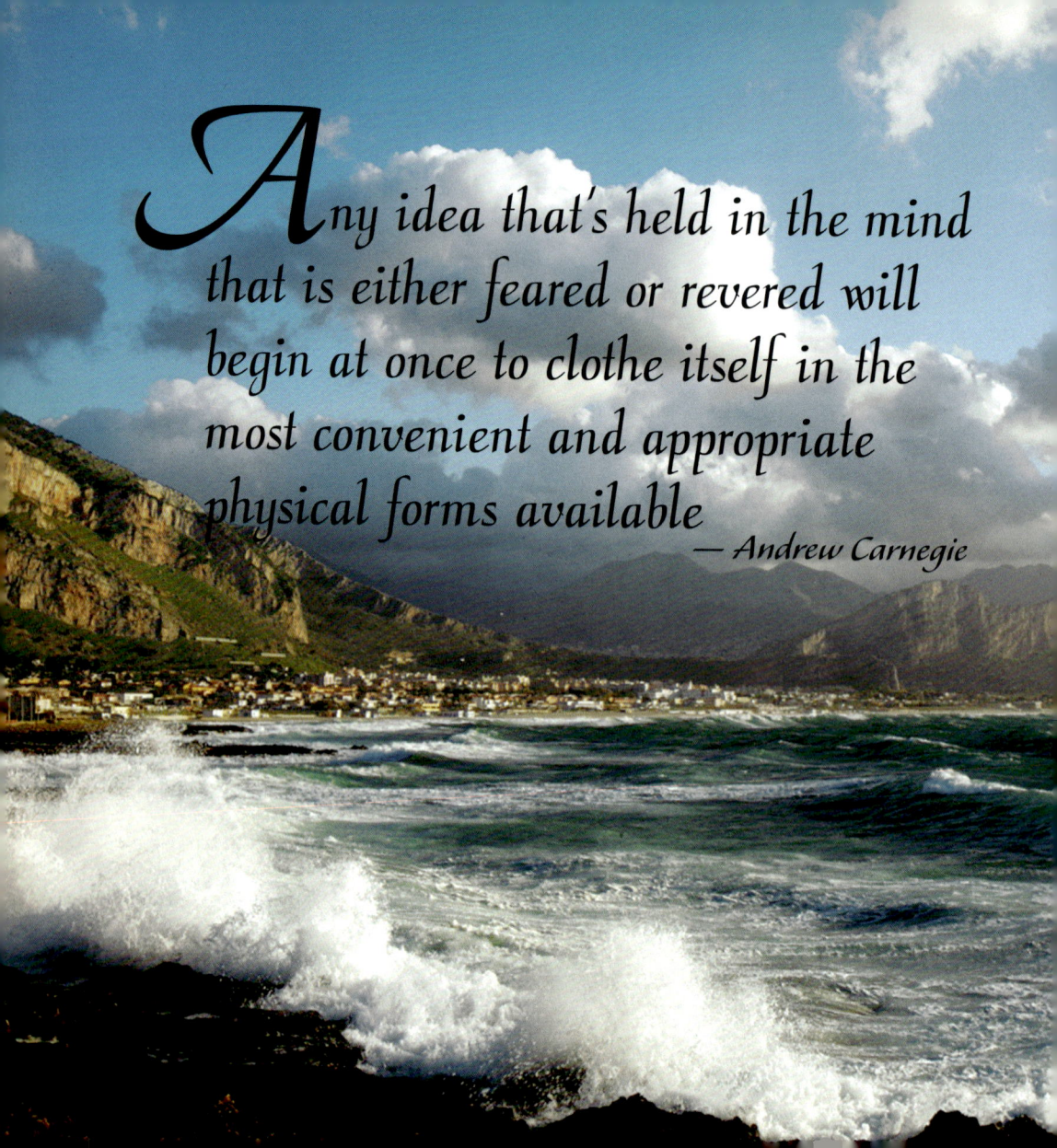

Any idea that's held in the mind that is either feared or revered will begin at once to clothe itself in the most convenient and appropriate physical forms available

— Andrew Carnegie

Without Desire, there would be no focus to your actions or energy. When you focus all your energy and positive thinking on your Desire, you will be working to make that Desire a reality. That's not to say, however, you can make everything you want happen all at once. To turn just one of your wants into a reality, you need to concentrate a significant amount of your intellectual and emotional energy.

To do this: sort through your thoughts until you can pinpoint your foremost Desire. Once you have isolated this idea, think about what has to happen in order for this Desire to become a reality. What are you willing to give up to see this happen? When can you reasonably expect to achieve this goal? What actions will you take toward achieving this end?

In answering these questions, you will create a clear path to your Desire. It may be helpful to write down exactly what you will do and when you will do it as you move forward. That way, before you even set foot on the path toward achieving your Desire, you will understand

The only thing that will grow is the thing we give energy to

— *Emerson*

how each element of your plan fits into place and how it will help you to accomplish your desired end.

Next, write out a statement of exactly what it is you mean to accomplish. Start your commitment statement with: I am so happy and grateful now that: Name and describe your Desire clearly so you will always be able to form a perfect picture of it in your mind. Read this statement aloud to yourself every morning when you wake up and every night before you go to bed. This will serve to keep your Desire at the forefront of your mind at all times.

Earl Nightingale said, "Start to work toward your goal, and your goal will start to move toward you."

Focus all your energy on your idea and you will begin to attract everything you want into your life. Do something every day that moves you closer to achieving your Desire. It does not have to be a big thing, but it should be something you do every day. In that way, you will ensure

*Let the beauty of the world
Leave imprints on your heart*

— Maria Holmes

your attention stays focused and you keep the momentum of your energies moving forward.

(If you are not yet aware of your Desire, the proper path will be shown to you in time.)

Visualization

Once you have your Desire firmly in your mind, you can begin applying the principle of Visualization to it. Visualization is a powerful and essential tool in this process because it forces you to create a clear image of the end you are trying to achieve. It is much easier to believe you can get somewhere when you know what that place looks like and what steps you need to take along the way.

There are several elements that go into creating a functioning Visualization system. Begin by forming a clear picture in your mind of exactly what it is you are after — the car you want to drive, the house you want to

What lies behind us
And what lies before us
Are but small matters
Compared to what lies within us
— *Ralph Waldo Emerson*

live in, the lover you want to attract, or the professional position you want to achieve.

Once that is done and you can see clearly what you are after, you can begin to attach an emotional response to the image. Think about your Desire and focus on how it will make you feel to achieve it. Your emotional energy is a powerful force. It will connect you in new and dramatic ways to the Universe around you and will have a dynamic impact on the future you are trying to create for yourself.

Even more than that, Visualization is the bridge, the mechanism by which our inner world is linked with the outer world. Once this bridge is in place, it will be possible for your inner world to flow smoothly into the outer world all around you. The more powerful the emotional response to your Desire, the more quickly your bridge will be built and the easier it will be for your positive energies to move out into the Universe.

I am only one
But still I am one
I cannot do everything
But still I can do something

I will not refuse to do something
I can do something

— Helen Keller

In addition to creating a clear picture in your mind, you can also take several other steps to increase the power of your emotional response. For instance, affirmations and music are effective at amplifying emotions and bringing positive ones to the surface. It is important you incorporate daily affirmations and uplifting or inspirational music into your regular routine to maximize the effectiveness of your Visualization.

The importance of music in this process cannot be overlooked. While your emotional responses will certainly be enhanced by your musical exposure, it will also allow you to focus more directly on Desire. Attaching a musical trigger to your Visualization will make it easier for you to call up the image of what you are working toward, and keep it real and fresh in your mind.

My mentor, Bob Proctor, says, "You are God's highest form of creation. You are a living, breathing, creative magnet. You have the ability to control what you attract into your life.

*The greatest way into
the Universe
Is through gratitude*
— Maria Holmes

1. Visualize your end result.

2. Ask for what you desire.

3. The answer will come to you in the form of inspired opportunity.

4. Believe that you will receive and you deserve it.

5. When it does, <u>act</u> on it.

Gratitude

By recognizing and maintaining your Gratitude for all of the good things you already have in your life, you will generate a great deal of positive energy around all you are and all you hope to create.

Gratitude keeps you connected to your source of supply.

Author Melodie Beattie writes, "Gratitude unlocks the fullness of life... it makes sense of our past, brings peace for today, and creates a vision for tomorrow."

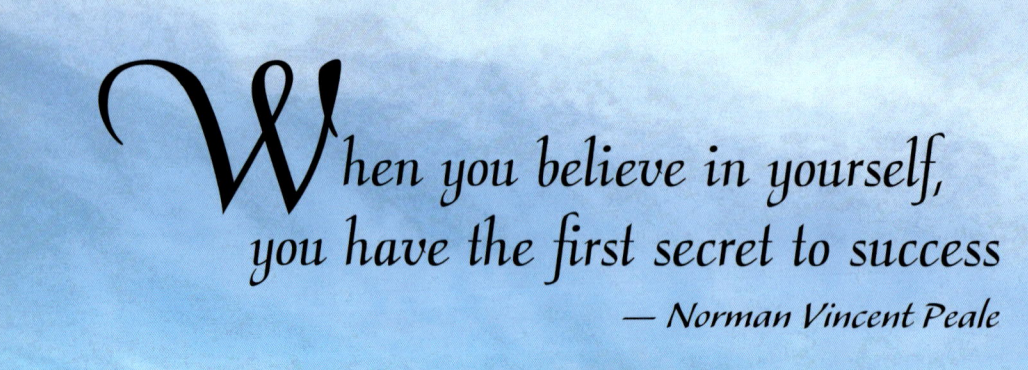

When you believe in yourself,
you have the first secret to success

— Norman Vincent Peale

The Law of Attraction does not work by allowing you to forcibly impose your will on the Universe to get what you want. Instead, it allows you to work in harmony with the other Universal energies around you to influence the course of events. In order to create this harmony, however, you must be able to see all of the blessings you have already been given and feel Gratitude for them.

Belief

You may master all of the other principles of the Law of Attraction, but unless you also have the Belief in yourself, your abilities, and in the Law of Attraction itself, you will not be able to make use of its power. Belief is what allows you to direct your energy in the right direction to make your Desire a reality.

When you are aware of your desire, it will manifest only at the level that you believe. When you are devoted, the Universe will align to give you what you desire.

Remember these words from the Sermon on the Mount, keep them constantly before you.

"Ask, and it shall be given you;
seek, and ye shall find;
knock, and it shall be opened unto you.
For everyone that asketh receiveth;
and he that seeketh findeth;
and to him that knocketh
it shall be opened."

Dr. Robert Schuller said, "Every achiever I have ever met says, 'My life turned around when I began to believe in me.'"

Faith

Faith is a principle closely linked to Belief and Gratitude, but it is also a significant element on its own. Your Faith in the Law of Attraction and the relationship between all of the elements of the Universe is what will give you the strength to persevere even in the face of overwhelming odds. It is not enough that your Desire is strong and your Gratitude plentiful.

You must also be able to fall back on your Faith to keep you going when things become difficult or challenging. Only through perseverance can you ultimately realize the end you have been seeking all along, no matter how incredible it may seem. True Faith gives you the courage to Believe when everyone else tells you it can't be done.

I matter to myself and others
I am a significant person
With incredible potential
and abilities

— Maria Holmes

As Clarence Smithson said, "Faith is the ability to see the invisible, to believe in the incredible, and to receive the impossible." By cultivating a true and pure Faith, you will make all things possible for yourself because of the immense wealth of positive energy you have to draw from.

I often hear that one person cannot change the world, but I am reminded that one person has changed my world. If you can share the awareness and truth of the Law of Attraction with only one person, you can change a life.

*I greet every person with a silent wish
For their health, happiness, and blessings*

— Maria Holmes

Chapter 4 | Choice

You Have the Power to Take the Next Step

When you can see and understand the significance of all of these principles, you will be ready to step forward and claim the life you've always dreamed of. All you need is the strength and guidance found in the Law of Attraction and to implement it effectively.

The Law of Attract is not a flight-of-fancy or a make-believe exercise. It is an unchanging, Universal Law, grounded in science, which makes everything happen in your life. By following these simple steps, you will be able to effect real and powerful change. Do it consistently, every moment of every day.

*Retain your vision,
stick to your purpose,
maintain your faith and gratitude*
— Wallace D. Wattle

1. Live in a state of Gratitude.

2. Use prayer, affirmations, and meditation daily.

3. Focus on the positive and see the good in everything and everyone with whom you come in contact.

4. Believe in the Universe. Believe in the source of your energy.

5. Write down your goal, take <u>action</u> toward it every day, and look at it or repeat it to yourself several times each day.

6. Create and believe in your vision. Actively visualize the life you deserve for ten minutes every morning, and again for ten minutes before you go to bed each night.

7. Purposefully create habits that make you feel good. This will, in turn, keep your energy levels high and your interaction with

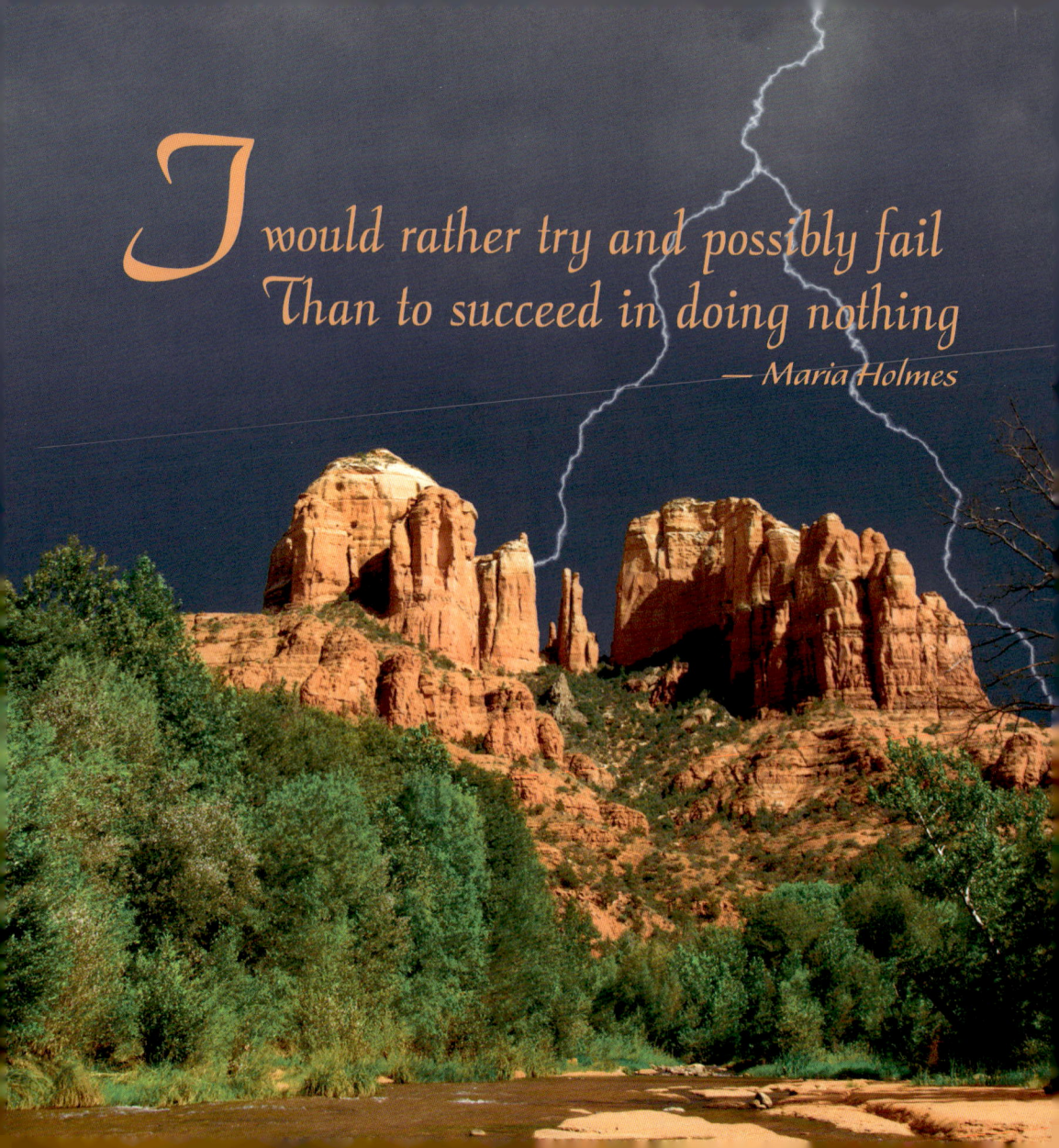

*I would rather try and possibly fail
Than to succeed in doing nothing*

— Maria Holmes

the Universal energy all around you at peak levels. Remember, once you have created momentum, it will continue to build in the direction you have laid out for it.

Your integrity is your destiny
It is the light that guides
your way

— Heraclitur

Chapter 5 | Manifest

Beyond the Myth of Fortune Telling

It is likely you have experienced the effects of the Law of Attraction in your own life. Have you ever been to a fortune-teller, mystic, or other spiritual person? Have you had your future read in tea leaves, coffee grounds, or Tarot cards? Have the predictions come true? Do you know someone who has had these experiences?

If you answered "yes" to any or all of these questions, you actually have your own proof that the Law of Attraction is a reality. Rather than look into the future and tell you what they saw, these fortune-tellers

Opportunities often come disguised in the form of misfortune or temporary defeat

— Napoleon Hill

merely planted an idea in your mind. You embraced the idea, believing it would happen, and your Belief made it a reality.

You were probably not even aware of it at the time, but you were interacting with and manipulating the energies of the Universe to generate the end you sought. And you only souyht it because the fortune-teller gave you a reason to believe it could come true. They gave you the power to have Faith that what they told you would come to pass. And so, you manifested it into reality.

*I am the creator of my life
And I succeed in everything I do*

— Maria Homes

Chapter 6 | Results

The Answer is Within You

The key to implementing the Law of Attraction is realizing you attract and create your own reality. You have the ability to shape your own future through your thoughts and beliefs. The results you desire will become your reality when you realize you can simply choose to make them so. This is not an easy or quick process, but it is effective.

If you truly desire to take charge of your life and create the future you deserve, take these principles to heart and incorporate them into your life. When you do this, you will be happier in the life you have now and be able to look with confidence to the even better future within reach.

*If one advances confidently in the direction of his dream
And endeavors to live the life he has imagined
He will meet with success unexpected in common hours*

— Henry David Thoreau

In addition, the ripples of outgoing positive energy you release will come back to you as waves, bringing all manner of good and unexpected things with them.

When you choose to live in harmony with the Universe and explore the powerful connections between every element of it, there will be no end to the amazing things you can accomplish and the positive experiences you'll have along the way.

2010

I thank the Universe every day for my blessings

— Maria Holmes

Affirmation

"I trust my highest good and greatest joy are unfolding now.

I trust God to show me the next step in my progress.

I am thankful for the awareness, and insight, and the knowledge this material has brought into my life...."

— Maria Holmes

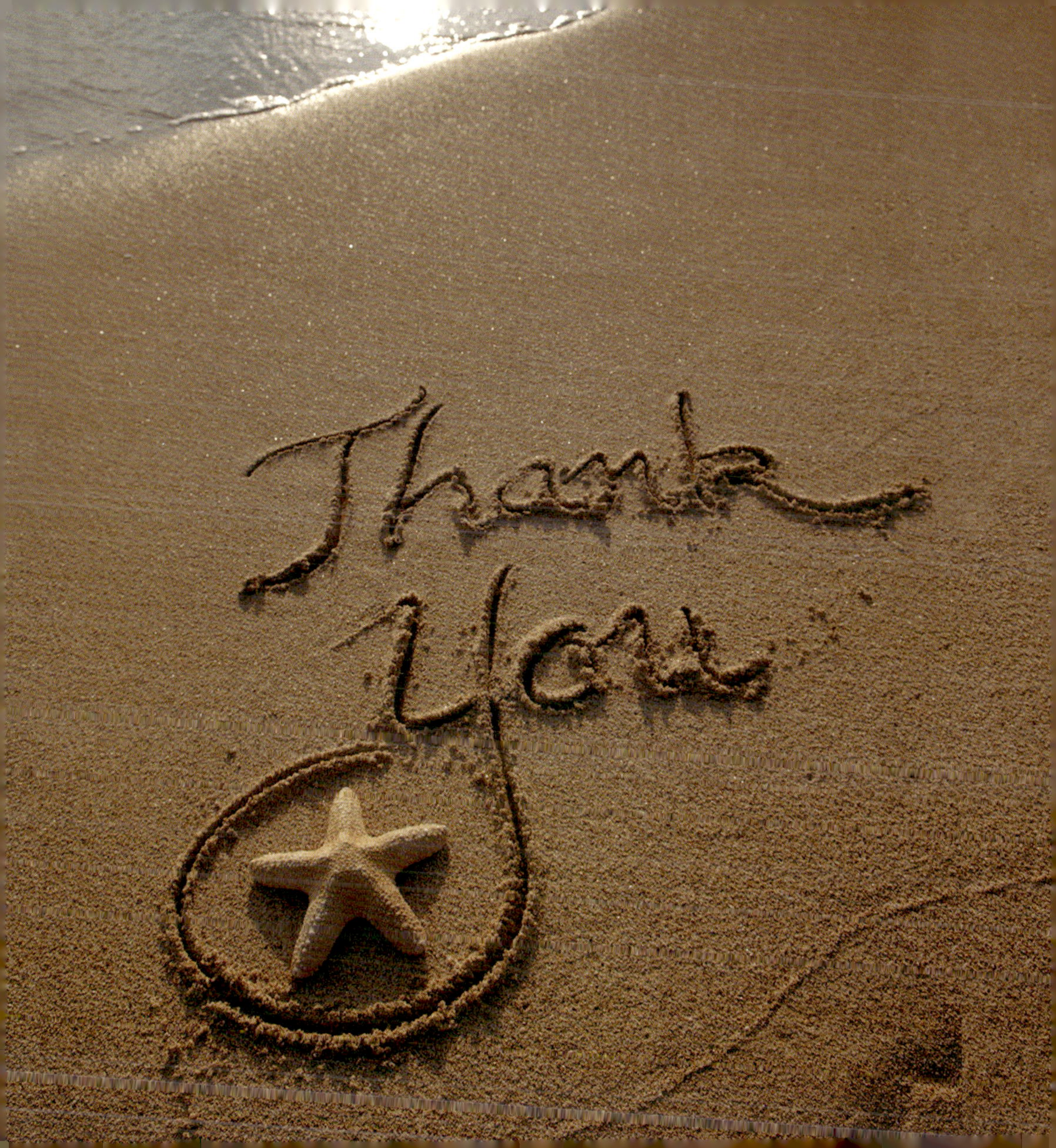
Thank You

About The Author...

A passionate advocate for the Law of Attraction, Maria began her journey twenty years ago, with the works of Deepak Chopra, and the *Celestine Prophesy*. After graduating from Indiana University with a Bachelor's Degree in Science, she studied with Anthony Robbins, Dr. Wayne Dyer, and Bob Proctor. Born in Greece and raised in Stuttgart, Germany by traditional Greek parents, Maria was exposed at an early age to the ancient art of coffee grind reading. Her mother was considered an expert in coffee grind reading and believed she was able to forecast events and upcoming information though the translation and understanding of the symbols. As Maria began her study of the Law of Attraction, she discovered it is one's belief in the future-reading that manifests the outcome, not the reader's "forecast." If you believe in the forecast then you create it in your life; you manifest it through the Law of Attraction. Maria's passion is to inspire and help others to understand how to use the Law of Attraction for a more joyful, fulfilled, and prosperous life.